I HATE MEN

I
HATE
MEN

Pauline Harmange

Translated by Natasha Lehrer

4th ESTATE • *London*

4th Estate
An imprint of HarperCollins*Publishers*
1 London Bridge Street
London SE1 9GF

www.4thEstate.co.uk

First published in Great Britain in 2020 by 4th Estate

First published in France as *Moi les hommes, je les déteste* by
Monstrograph, Collection Bootleg, in 2020

21 22 23 24 LSC 10 9 8 7 6 5 4 3 2 1

The chapter title 'I am woman, hear me roar' is taken from the song
'I am Woman' by Helen Reddy and Ray Burton.
Lyrics © Universal Music Publishing Group, BMG Rights Management

A catalogue record for this book is available from the British Library

ISBN 978-0-00-845758-7 (hardback)

Printed and bound in the United States of America by LSC Communications

Contents

One day I wrote on my blog that I was fed up of men's apathy and general lack of interest when it comes to women's rights. Almost immediately an anonymous lurker left a comment: 'Maybe you should ask yourself why men don't want to talk about it. A few possibilities: *the aggressive – hate-filled, even – attitude of feminists towards any man who doesn't say "I'm ashamed to be a man! Down with men!" The day you accept the relationship between men and women for what it is – then we'll listen to you. In the meantime, you're just going to be dismissed as sex-starved shrews, and you'll keep doing a disservice to your cause.*'

With these words, this delightful gentleman was making a barely veiled accusation of misandry against me. I'm far from the only woman charged with manhating: plenty of feminists and lesbians are repeatedly accused of such an affront.

As though challenging male power, or simply not being attracted to men, constitutes nothing more than hatred.

The accusation of misandry is a mechanism for silencing women, a way of silencing the anger – sometimes violent but always legitimate – of the oppressed standing up to their oppressors. Taking offence at misandry, claiming it's merely a form of sexism like any other, and no less unacceptable (as if sexism were genuinely reviled), is a bad-faith way of sweeping under the carpet the mechanisms that make sexist oppression a systemic phenomenon buoyed throughout history by culture and authority. It's to allege that a woman who hates men is as dangerous as a man who hates women – and that there's no rational justification for what she feels, be it dislike, distrust or disdain. Because, obviously, no man has ever hurt a woman in the whole course of human history. Or rather, no *men* have ever hurt any *women*.

As a result of the way it's been misunderstood or misconstrued, there's a tendency in feminist movements to argue that misandry as a concept doesn't actually exist. In a way, of course, this is true, because there is no coordinated, structured system for denigrating or coercing men. And because even when we do sometimes put all our messieurs in one basket, it's more to laugh at them, it's kind of tongue in cheek, if you know what I mean. Honestly, we're very nice, underneath it all.

But what if misandry were necessary – healthy, even? I get why women reject it. It's unnerving to be accused of being a horrid extremist who hates men. Thousands of women were burned at the stake for less.

But you know what? I'm going to have a go. I'll admit it: I hate men. All of them, really? Yes, the whole lot of them. By default, I have very little respect for any of them. Which is funny actually, because ostensibly I don't have any legitimacy when it comes to hating men. I chose to marry one, after all, and I have to admit that I'm still very fond of him.*

That doesn't, however, stop me from wondering why men are as they are. They're violent, selfish, lazy and cowardly. It doesn't stop me wondering why we women are supposed graciously to accept their flaws – what am I saying, I mean their deficiencies – even though men beat, rape and murder us. *Boys will be boys.* Girls, on the other hand, will become women, and will learn to make their peace with this, because there's no way to escape the narrow vision of our destiny as refracted through the crystal ball of the patriarchy. *Come on, we're perfectly capable of putting up with their little idiosyncrasies.* In any case, we don't have a choice.

---

* My choice can't be taken entirely out of context, however. As a bisexual woman, I have no idea what my life might have been like if I hadn't been confronted early on by homophobia, both among the people that I knew and in wider society.

What kind of woman are you if you avoid the male gaze? Take your choice: sex-starved, dyke, or hysteric.

Apart from the fact that it undermines our cause, it appears that misandry is also very difficult for men to deal with – an intolerable brutality that adds up to the shocking outrage of precisely zero deaths and zero casualties. Apparently, what with all this feminist bullshit, #MeToo and the rest of that crap, it's very hard to be a man nowadays. They don't know how to flirt any more, how to get in a lift with their female colleagues, how to crack a joke. What *do* they still have the right to do now?

So much existential dread, for which I don't feel a great deal of sympathy. All that time they spend snivelling about how hard it is to be a poor persecuted man nowadays is just a way of adroitly shirking their responsibility to make themselves a little less the pure products of the patriarchy.

Strangely, not many men actually stop to wonder why feminists dislike them so much – if they did they might notice the statistics are quite damning. But they're too busy explaining to us that *they're* not like that, that it's really not nice to generalise like that. And if we alienate them with all that talk of *men are trash*, the risk is they won't join in and *help us* in our struggle. As if we were incapable of organising our struggle without them, as if we haven't been doing precisely that for years – and as if, when they invited themselves into our ranks to join the struggle, they didn't always end up taking over, talking over us and even imposing their decisions on us while they were about it.

I see misandry as a potential way out. A way of refusing to accept these norms, of saying *no* with every breath. Hating men as a social group, and sometimes as individuals too, brings me so much joy – and not just because I'm a crazy old cat lady.

If we all became misandrists, what a fabulous hue and cry we could raise. We'd realise (though it might be a bit sad at first) that we don't actually need men. I believe too we might liberate an unsuspected power: that of being able to soar far above the male gaze and the dictates of men, to discover at last who we really are.

Misandry, a definition

I think at this point it's worth defining the concept
of misandry as I employ it in this essay. I use the
word misandry to mean a negative feeling towards
the entirety of the male sex. This negative feeling
might be understood as a spectrum that ranges
from simple suspicion to outright loathing, and
is generally expressed by an impatience towards
men and a rejection of their presence in women's
spaces. And when I say 'the male sex' I mean all
the cis men who have been socialised as such, and
who enjoy their male privilege without ever calling
it into question, or not enough (yes, misandry is a
demanding and elitist concept).

Ultimately, misandry is a principle of pre-
caution. Having spent so much time being at best

disappointed and at worst abused by men – all the more so having absorbed the feminist theory that articulates patriarchy and sexism – it's quite natural to develop a carapace and stop opening up to the first man who comes along and swears on his heart that he's a really good guy.* All the more so given that to prove his worth, the man in question simply has to demonstrate genuine thoughtfulness in order for our hostile feelings to subside. But his probation period will last forever: nothing against him personally, it's just that it's hard to give up privilege, and even more so to actively campaign for all one's fellow men to be similarly stripped of theirs. He might be feeling a bit low one day and

* A little observation with no scientific basis: most of the time when a man goes on about how decent he is, you only have to scratch the surface for the veneer to begin to crack. It's a bit like that old cliché about sex itself, except in this case it's true – the ones who go on about it the most are the least likely to be actually doing it.

be tempted to hit on a girl in a bar who's already made it very clear that she's not interested. A lousy day at the office, and he's back to his bad habit of shameless mansplaining and interrupting you every five minutes. We need to be vigilant, we have to keep our eye on even the genuinely decent ones, because anyone can stray off course, and all the more so if he's cis, white, wealthy, able-bodied and heterosexual. The sum of his privilege is so great that it makes him very resistant to change. We need men to be exemplary in their behaviour, because when we women speak, no one listens. We simply can't afford to let them get away with doing things half-heartedly.

The very least a man can do when faced with a woman who expresses misandrist ideas is shut up and listen. He'd learn a great deal and emerge a better person. He might even agree, in the end. But beware of the man who slopes off in the other direction, and starts beating himself up with a great wailing and gnashing of teeth; no woman, and certainly no misandrist, has the slightest desire to listen to a man bemoaning his lot as a privileged male, playing the martyr. I'm yet to come across a man who claims to be a misandrist, but I'm pretty sure if I did it would have the same effect on me as when I hear a man declare himself a feminist. Feminist activists have always had an instinctive suspicion of and tendency to reject these men. Many of us believe that men can't be feminists, that they have no right to appropriate a term that was forged by the oppressed. It's extraordinarily common for men who like to trumpet the fact that they are feminists to have failed to deconstruct their privilege as much as they'd like us to think, and to blithely take advantage of it to trample on and abuse the women in their lives. There is nothing more tedious than to see a man being covered in plaudits that are completely disproportionate to the minuscule effort he makes, while women continue to be subject to impossible standards that mean they're always the ones to lose out. We have to stop praising men for such pathetically trivial things as leaving work early to pick up their kid from school. Do not forget that in exactly the same situation a woman is blamed and criticised, whatever her choice.

Hang on, though: I'm not saying that men shouldn't be interested in feminism, nor that they shouldn't try to understand the struggle and share its values. Quite the opposite: what I resent is their not being interested enough, or feigning an interest for the wrong reasons (because they fancy a feminist, for example – just don't go there). There's a whole world of difference between 'understanding the mechanisms of oppression and one's own place in the system', and 'appropriating it in order to take centre stage and make it all about yourself yet again'. What we want is for men to put their power and privilege to good use: by policing their male friends and acquaintances, for example, instead of explaining to women how to go about fighting their battles. We want men to know their place. Actually no, what we really want is for them to learn how to take up less space. They don't get to play the lead, and they're going to have to get used to that.

If I like to highlight the correspondence between misandry and feminism, it's for the simple reason that it took me several years of moving in feminist circles to develop my dislike of men, to be comfortable with it, and to stop trying to hide it, even in the company of my close male friends. It was, I think, the regular practice of feminism that allowed me to develop a basic level of assertiveness and self-confidence. You become far less forgiving when you analyse the statistics on violence against women through the prism of sociology. Now we recognise that what we experience within the types of relationships that are usually considered private and personal also has a political dimension. These experiences are systemic; it's not that we've lost our minds because we love making a drama out of everything.

At last we've woken up to the fact that we're not alone, whether we're being wolf-whistled in the street, or assaulted* by some guy we thought we could trust, or because we're stuck inside keeping the home fires burning; the reason we're fed up isn't because we're the weaker sex, or because we've got an aggressive temperament, but because of a profound sense of an injustice of which we are all victim.

I've noticed a similar pattern among many of my female friends and acquaintances in terms of their relationship to both feminism and misandry. They start out as fairly apolitical feminists '*à la française*' (which is to say very keen to recognise the problem of equality between the sexes in other countries, but generally inclined to conclude that

---

* Here I'm referring not only to physical violence, assault and rape, but also to symbolic violence such as, for example, the widely accepted view that women don't have the right kind of minds or the necessary skills to become good managers.

things in France are mostly okay, we don't have too much to complain about), but as they begin to dig a little deeper, to investigate a bit more, they become increasingly outraged at the situation, both here and elsewhere, and to feel a deep sense of anger. As they delve more deeply, they can no longer ignore the evidence – the fact that men and masculinity are a problem, undoubtedly for the whole of society, but particularly for women. This is how they become misandrists. Because there simply aren't very many other options, and because, once they've had their eyes opened to the profound mediocrity of the majority of men, there's no good reason to carry on liking them by default.

Shacking up with a man

One day, during a discussion with some girlfriends about the strange habit men have of believing themselves to be excellent lovers without ever bothering to enquire about their partner's satisfaction, I let slip the trope *men are trash* one too many times. One of the participants in the debate turned to me and said, in essence: 'Okay, seriously, enough of this bullshit. It's easy for you to say, surprise, surprise, because your boyfriend's perfect! Shut the fuck up.' At the time, I really didn't know how to respond to my hypocrisy being flagged up like this.

As it happens, I'm pretty certain that were I to find myself single tomorrow, it would be very difficult for me to begin a new relationship with a man. I'd never have the energy to start all over again with someone I didn't know, and I'd be a lot less tolerant today about things that used to seem perfectly natural, and apparently still do for plenty of men (and women), that my partner and I have worked hard together to deconstruct.

I was almost seventeen when I met the person who became my husband, and at the time it would never have occurred to me to hate men. Men were essential to the way I saw myself. Their opinions were the only ones that mattered: however many times a girlfriend might tell me I was pretty (or clever, but I didn't care so much about that), no man apart from my father ever confirmed it, so I didn't believe it for a second. Was I slim enough, nicely dressed enough, dared I dream that one day they might like me? I was profoundly convinced that they would not, and that in all likelihood I would die alone, without ever having been in love. With a head filled to overflowing with the romantic nonsense with which little girls are indoctrinated, I was, clearly, excessively dramatic, but it was obvious that boys of my age were swanning about as though they both performed and expected sex (which I didn't really want to give them, but if I had to go that far so as not to be cast away like a sock full of holes, I guessed I would) at the expense of love. That's precisely what every girl that age is warned of, and what's expected of every boy. We deny them any emotions.

I was lucky enough to meet someone who didn't try to coerce me into having sex with him, and who wasn't afraid to admit that he too wanted to fall in love. I didn't like myself much when I was seventeen, and I'd had a few brushes with some nasty characters (how boring they were really) who'd hurt me, sometimes without me even realising. I was certainly no feminist. In fact I hadn't yet formed much in the way of my own opinions. Nor had my boyfriend: we began the process of (de)constructing ourselves together and since then our ways of seeing the world have continued to correspond.

Not that I want to be disloyal, but I have to be honest: my beloved isn't *perfect*. He doesn't rape me, he doesn't hit me, he does the dishes and the vacuuming, he treats me with the respect I deserve. Is that what it means to be perfect? Or is it just the least one might expect? Are standards so low that men are really allowed to get off so lightly?

To be fair, I'm not perfect either. Nobody is. It just seems to me that women's efforts to make themselves more pleasing to their spouses are rarely reciprocated.

We go into therapy, we read books to learn how to be more organised, how to relax, how to orgasm, we talk about our feelings, we initiate dialogue, we do sport, go on diets, have makeovers and cosmetic surgery, we get coaching, change jobs; we tie ourselves up in knots in a never-ending process of self-improvement.

With my yoga mat, my meditation app, my two different kinds of therapy, my books about non-violent communication and my relative ability to control my sometimes overwhelming emotions, I feel like such a cliché. I remember once explaining to my husband the principles of non-violent communication, hoping that it would offer us a way to express disagreement without immediately lapsing into a stormy argument. He could have read the book I bought too. Or he could even – what a mad idea! – have taken the initiative, acknowledged that we never manage to resolve our arguments satisfactorily, and come up with some kind of solution himself. But that's never what happens. I'm the one who shoulders the entire emotional burden of the relationship. That's what women do, because in a heterosexual relationship it's always the woman who's learned to do that. Of course, men could learn to do it too, but it's a bit like learning a foreign language: it's that much harder once you're an adult, and if there's already someone there prepared to make the effort to speak the other person's language, why bother?

Even though I love my husband and have never thought for a second of leaving him, I continue to reflect and insist upon my dislike of men. And to tar him with the same brush. I can do that, because life isn't simple, and I experience both the particular and the general.

On the one hand, I am witness on a daily basis to the decency of this man in particular, and the immense effort he makes. It's not always enough, progress can be heavy going, but it is worth it. I still reproach him for his habit of waiting for me to offer up my pre-digested concepts and reflections about masculinity, rather than deconstructing his own as much as he can; and for the way he interrupts me, can't bear to be wrong, and doesn't make more of an effort to listen to and support me when I'm stressed or upset. All of these habits are intimately linked to masculinity.

If I refuse to grant him the right to be mediocre because he's a man and that's what men are like, it's because I want to grant myself the same respect that I have for all women, for whom I wish truly egalitarian relationships.

The thing is, I don't live in a bubble, cut off from the world and the rest of society. Every day I'm witness to the immense indifference that men have for women. I read statistics about rape, harassment, femicide; I observe debates on social media and listen to the conversations with men I come across or interact with. The decisions taken by male politicians, the words used to describe us by male artists. Sexist jokes that still make people bellow with laughter. I know that behind every man who is even slightly conscious of his male privilege are several women who have worked hard to help him open his eyes – yet how few men recognise this. And I know that there are still far too many men whose eyes remain desperately, obstinately closed.

23

Hysterical and sexually frustrated misandrists

Women don't want to think of themselves as misandrists, and when they do use the word it's with a heavy irony which they almost always want to emphasise. They seem to want to reassure (themselves), to make it clear that they're only joking, they don't *really* hate men. And this is how the gulf is opened up that separates the systemic oppression that is patriarchy from the slight dent to the ego that a misandrist insult represents. We aren't hurting anyone when we hate men. And, for that matter, we don't really hate them, because we've all got boyfriends, brothers, fathers, sons, colleagues and friends whom we like and love.

But it's clear that many women feel uncomfortable at the idea of stating loud and clear, even in women-only spaces, a dislike or mistrust of men in general.

To start with, people ask themselves whether misandry isn't in fact totally counter-productive, from a feminist perspective. Surely it only harms our cause, proving to our opponents and detractors that feminists are indeed sexually frustrated, irrational and vindictive hysterics? What's the point of alienating all men? Don't we want them to be our allies?

Looked at from the point of view of being a woman, it's similarly complicated. Conflict and anger are not tools and emotions that we tend naturally to be able to control: we're brought up to be docile little girls who will grow up to become gentle and understanding women. To announce point blank that one doesn't like men is to personify an anger that is far larger than our own selves, and to lay ourselves open to confrontation – with society in general, which gives so much space to men, their idiosyncrasies and their crimes; and with individual men, if they're not prepared to listen to how we feel.

I have a few ideas for how to respond to these legitimate questions.

First, do we actually need the approbation of those – so often men – who claim our criticism is over the top, in order to believe that our words are valid? If our misandry alienates us from men who can't cope with our anger, are they really worth our time? Do they deserve our efforts? There are men who have agreed to listen to the reasons why our relationships with them are skewed, why their privilege must be deconstructed, and who don't start squawking the minute they hear someone say that all men are bastards. They get it, they even agree. They are our allies, not the men who elbow us out of the way to get to the front of the feminist stage and refuse to take responsibility for their problematic behaviour.

Anger and violence are often conflated, though the two don't necessarily go hand in hand. Anger at being treated as an inferior is not remotely comparable to the violence committed by the men who humiliate, rape and kill us, or even the violence committed by the men who ignore us, turn their backs on us and mock us. We have everything to gain by distancing ourselves from the limited role of the patient, gentle, almost passive woman, and insisting that men make the effort to become better people.

That's why I'm no longer prepared to rush to reassure everyone, whether online or in real life, that in fact no, I'm not really a misandrist, I wouldn't dream of suggesting that we'd be better off without the influence – even without the presence – of men in our lives. The fact is, I'm not joking at all when I say I'm a misandrist, so why should I pretend I am? I have no desire any more to waste my time and my energy pretending to be sweet and pleasant. Perhaps I'm just not – and at the end of the day, it doesn't really matter.

Men who hate women

You don't have to go as far as declaring yourself a misandrist to be at the receiving end of a slew of attacks about the way in which you express your criticism of the male sex. You just have to make a few generalisations, say 'men' instead of 'some men' – even when in plenty of cases it seems perfectly justified to generalise – and congratulations, you're a misandrist! And if you're a misandrist, you deserve no better than a misogynist. In the collective imagination, misandry and misogyny are two sides of the same coin, that of sexism. The problem is, I suppose, the etymology: drawn from the same root, both words presumably cover the same principles? Well, actually, no they don't. Life's funny like that.

If misandry is a characteristic of someone who hates men, and misogyny that of someone who hates women, it has to be conceded that in reality, the two concepts are not equal, either in terms of the dangers posed to their targets or the means used to express them. (Let's not forget that misogynists use weapons ranging from online abuse to deadly attacks, like the one that took place at the École Polytechnique in Montreal in 1989, or Elliot Rodger's 2014 killing spree in Isla Vista, California, that have never yet seen their misandrist equivalents.) Misandry and misogyny cannot be compared, quite simply because the former exists only in reaction to the latter.

You'd literally have to have never looked beyond the end of your nose – or alternatively to be possessed of exceptional bad faith – to deny point blank that the violence women suffer is, in the huge majority of cases, perpetrated by men. This isn't a matter of opinion, it's a fact. The reason society is patriarchal is because there are men who use their male privilege to the detriment of the other half of the population. Some of this violence is insidious, background noise in the daily lives of women, so pernicious that we grow up with the impression that it's the norm in male/female relationships. Other kinds of violence are so shocking that they make the headlines in national newspapers.

In 2017 in France, 90 per cent of the people who received death threats from their partners were women,[1] while 86 per cent of those murdered by their partner or ex-partner were also women. Of the sixteen women who killed their partner, at least eleven, that is, 69 per cent of them, had themselves been victims of domestic violence.[2] In 2019, 149 women were murdered by their partner or their former partner. In 2018, 96 per cent of those who received a prison sentence for domestic violence were men, and 99 per cent of those sentenced for sexual violence were men.[3]

It's not only women who are the victims of sexual attacks and rape, though it's hard to find statistics of sexual attacks on men.* There's an enormous taboo when it comes to talking about sexual violence perpetrated against men, who suffer the full force of sexist stereotypes that imply that a man cannot be raped, since supposedly they're always up for sex. It's also very difficult for men to talk about sexual trauma. Society expects them to be strong and virile: nothing can be forced on them – and if it is, they aren't 'real' men.

A significant number of rapes are committed against minors, both male and female,[4] and here too, the perpetrators are overwhelmingly men.[5]

---

* There is a large body of research in English on sexual attacks perpetrated against male prisoners, including by prison personnel, some of whom, though in smaller numbers, are women. This is another fact that reminds us of the extent to which rape is a question of power.

In fact, whatever the sex or age of the victim of sexual harassment or violence – whether male or female, child or adult – it is vital to emphasise that *the vast majority of those responsible for such violence are men.*

Clearly nowadays there are very few men shouting from the rooftops that they're misogynist or sexist. In fact, they often defend themselves against such accusations with inimitable eloquence: 'Me, sexist? I've got a wife, two daughters, two female cats and twenty hens. It's an all-female household.'* It's a well-known fact: you just have to surround yourself with women to be automatically cleansed of all sexism. It's rather frowned upon today to declare a dislike of women, or to expect them to be silent and docile. This makes it a bit trickier to spot the misogynist, if he isn't wearing

---

* This was the response of Philippe Fasan, deputy mayor of Montauban, in 2017, to accusations of sexism after a post on his Facebook page.

a shiny little badge. But you can still assume that a man who bullies, beats, rapes or kills a woman probably doesn't have a great deal of respect for her. You could also argue that any man who doesn't see the problem when other men bully, beat, rape and kill women probably doesn't like them much either. Fundamentally, any man who believes that the patriarchy is merely the fruit of the feminist imagination rather than a concrete reality is complicit in systemic sexism.

There are times when making a generalisation isn't an easy shortcut but a straightforward description of reality. In such a case you'd have to be deeply egocentric to respond with '*Not all men are rapists!*' when a woman lets slip that she's sick of men. It's true that not all men are rapists, but it's also true that almost all rapists are men – and almost all women have or will suffer some kind of violence at the hands of men. That's where the problem lies. That's the root of our loathing and distrust.

But it also lies with the men who don't rape, and all the other things they don't do either.

When they don't assume their share of the mental load, meaning that in the twenty-first century we're still overwhelmingly the ones responsible for the shopping, the kids and the emotional labour in our relationships. When they don't accord us our place in the public sphere, which they still monopolise as if it were an extension of their own living room, yielding us barely a small corner to sit in under their mocking glances.[6] When they refuse us our place in conversation too, by constantly interrupting us, patronising us with their answers, rephrasing our ideas so that they can steal them, closing their ears to whatever we're trying to say.

When they get together and laugh at sexist jokes because after all it's completely harmless. When they say that maybe she was asking for it, you never know, sometimes girls say no when they really mean yes.

There are plenty of reasons to dislike men, if you think about it. Reasons backed up by facts. Why do men hate women? During the thousands of years that men have benefited from their dominant social position, what did we do – *what have we done* – to deserve their violence?

Misandry has a target, but it doesn't have a list of victims whose morbid tally is totted up on almost a daily basis.* We don't injure or kill men, we don't prevent them from getting a job or following whatever their passion is, or dressing as they wish, or walking down the street after dark, or expressing themselves however they see fit. And when someone does give themselves the right to impose such things on men, that person is always a man, and it still falls within the hetero-patriarchal system.

---

* As the Collective of Feminicides by Their (Former) Partners has been doing since 2016, see @FeminicidesFR on Twitter.

We misandrists stay in our lane. We might hate men, but at best we put up with them, frostily, because they're everywhere and we don't have any choice (incredible but true: it's possible to hate someone without having an irrepressible urge to kill them). At worst we stop inviting them into our lives – or at least we make a drastic selection beforehand. Our misandry scares men, because it's the sign that they're going to have to start meriting our attention. Having relationships with men isn't something we owe them, a duty, but, as in every balanced relationship, all the parties involved have to make an effort to treat one another with respect.

As long as there are misogynistic men who don't give a damn, and a culture that condones and encourages them, there will be women who are so fed up they refuse to bear the brunt of exhausting or toxic relationships.

I am woman, hear me roar

I don't recall ever getting angry when I was a little girl. I must have done when I was a baby, but as a child people always said that I was good as gold. I think I understood very quickly that I wasn't allowed to be angry. None of the women around me ever got angry, nor any of the little girls. I say 'none of the women' because I'm not counting maternal anger directed towards children. This kind of anger is part of a complex system in which the mental burden and unequal division of labour related to the bringing up of children prompts more occasions for anger in the mother than in the father, who more often than not only takes an active role in the enjoyable aspects of parenthood.

My mother certainly knows how to be angry. She'll be the one who picks up the phone to complain to the internet provider, calmly explaining in glacial tones what's not working and what she needs, always ending up getting what she wants. She uses the same tone of voice with dishonest shopkeepers, or students who cheat and then deny they've cheated (she's a teacher), or with mean-minded colleagues . . . I used to call it her magic power, and only later – when I didn't dare take the same tone to demand my due in a social situation or when someone tried to cheat me – did I realise what a great power it is.

However, I think that when my mother's in conflict with those she's close to, those who matter to her (her husband, my father, for example), she struggles to express her anger. Like me, she grumbles then weeps, in a swift escalation of emotion that goes straight from irritation to floods of tears and ultimately fails to articulate anything very distinct. At least that's how I see it, for I often use the same technique with my own husband, and it's doomed to failure. Partly because it's difficult to communicate criticism or reproach to a person you love and live with, but also, perhaps, because it's difficult to convey criticism or reproach to a man, full stop.

Male anger is spectacular. It's all about shouting, and sometimes physical blows, most of the time against material objects – though not always, as is borne out by the number of women beaten by their partners. In short, men's anger is full of aggression. We encourage boys to be angry – always better than snivelling like a girl – and to fight back. In films, and sometimes in real life, when a boy is insulted, teased or punched by another boy at school, his father, or some other alpha male, encourages him to respond with physical violence: that's how you defend yourself when you're a boy.

When I was at secondary school, there was a girl in my class who took a real dislike to me, and one day for some reason she slapped me in front of the whole class, then turned around and walked away. If we'd been boys, all my friends would have encouraged me to hit her back, and it would have ended in the classic playground brawl. But we were girls and, after the initial shock on the part of both adults and other children at the violence of such a gesture *coming from a girl*, everyone advised me to forget about it. It never even crossed my mind to run after the girl and hit her back. I felt humiliated and sad. But I wasn't angry.

The examples we set in both cases are toxic; neither the violence we encourage in boys nor the passivity we impose on girls is an appropriate response, for ourselves or for other people, in situations of injustice or conflict. But then what alternatives should we propose, in order for our children's selves to be shaped differently?

I only discovered anger much later, after I became a feminist. I realised that often the things that made me cry ought to have made me yell, and that when in the course of an argument I wept with misery at the unfairness of it, I was in a way resigning myself to losing. I had to change in order to better serve my own interests: I learned to fight back. Not that all arguments are battlegrounds, but there are causes that deserve not to be abandoned. Of course, as soon as I began getting angry, people began to reproach me for it.

In private, domestic disputes between men and women are the archetypal examples of these different types of socialisation. Many people are incapable of handling conflict without raising their voices, for it's never pleasant to hear criticism being levelled against you. But the truth is there's no good means of expressing anger if you're a woman in a relationship with a man. If you weep as a way of articulating a kind of despair at a situation that seems dedicated to maintaining the status quo (which I have a tendency to do), you're being too emotional, or unnecessarily dramatic. If you get angry and try to express more clearly what's gone wrong and insist that things change, you'll be accused of being aggressive and no one will listen to you any more, with that age-old argument: 'I can't hear you when you shout like that.'

I get the impression, whenever I discuss this with other people, that in the case of heterosexual couples it's almost always the woman who picks domestic fights. Instead of interpreting this as the biological tendency of women to be constantly nagging and nitpicking, surely it would be better to think about the causes of these disputes. People might then recognise how often they're rooted in an attempt to balance out a deeply inequitable situation. And how the weight of the mental burden in a heterosexual relationship, where the tendency of a man is simply not to hear what his partner is telling him, means that a woman has no choice but to raise her voice. Criticising women for creating discord is dishonest as well as sexist.

In and of itself, conflict is no bad thing. Obviously it suggests there's a problem in the relationship, but at the same time it indicates a desire to get things out in the open in order to resolve them. When a conflict blows up within a straight relationship that's rooted in domestic dynamics, it's usually the woman who's upset and sounds the alarm, and the man who insists on hearing only the form of the quarrel, the crying and shouting, so that he can sweep away the reasons for it with the back of his hand. It's a way of refusing to listen to criticism, and thus of avoiding any soul-searching. Men who choose the terrain of reason, as opposed to emotion, place themselves in a position of authority. Only someone in a position of dominance can permit himself to be calm and reasonable in any circumstance, because he's not the one who is suffering. It's a choice not to hear the emotions of an interlocutor – the choice of not wanting to understand the other side of the story, and of refusing to envisage the possibility that one might bear any responsibility for it.

Of course, not every conflict in a straight relationship is due to the mental or emotional burden, just as not all men choose to block their ears in response to criticism from their partner. Nor am I suggesting that women are never at fault. But there's no doubt that there's a recurring motif in the increasing number of narratives emerging about the supposedly inconsequential details of daily life that stifle women – think of the Instagram accounts and newspaper articles that explore the challenge of being a feminist when you're in a relationship with a man.[7] These things that burden us are not the products of our imagination, whatever the men in our lives might say – and occasionally too the little voice inside our heads that would prefer us to take it on the chin instead of making waves.

Misandry is born out of and nourished by anger. Feminism is the interface between private anger, which belongs in the domestic space, and public anger; 'the personal is political', whether we're talking about the gender pay gap or which person in a couple has remembered to put on the washing. Yet for a very long time, women's anger struggled to express itself as feminist. The thing is, no one likes emotions spilling over, even less so when they're from a woman, and so it took a long time to reclaim this anger. Now it's begun to find its voice, and the taboos that have stifled it for centuries are being stripped away: people have started to write about it,* to reflect on its causes, to compare it to male anger. It *exists*. We must cherish this voice and feed the flames of our anger deep in our breasts, heed its calls for justice and reparations, its insistence that we not lose heart. Our anger insists that men take responsibility for their behaviour and spurs on our revolution.

---

* See for example *Libérer la colère (Liberate Anger)*, edited by Geneviève Morand and Natalie-Ann Roy, les éditions du remue-ménage, 2018.

Mediocre as a white dude

Once I'd gauged the extent of my anger towards men, I felt rather helpless. What to do about all those mediocre men I saw all around me? Didn't throwing them into the (non-recycling) bin risk creating a void in my life that would be impossible to fill? Was there any solution other than to go and live in an abandoned shack somewhere deep in a forest?

Here's the scoop, though: humanity isn't made up of only men. It's difficult to believe, given how much room they take up and the way they've managed to make everyone believe they're completely indispensable. But don't panic: once we've given men the push, we'll realise there's

a load of awesome women (starting with ourselves, obviously) that the noisy and damaging
ubiquity of men has kept us from noticing and
appreciating.

It's amazing how we manage to forget
about ourselves, simply because every day we're
overwhelmed by the sheer extent of male self-
aggrandisement. This isn't to say that all men are
necessarily malign, but it's hard to fight the idea
that's imprinted on our psyches very early on in
our lives that men's opinions, even those given
in passing on the street, are more valuable than
ours. Even those of us in relationships we think
of as egalitarian still police our way of being, how
we present ourselves to the world, to please the
men in our lives. We buy clothes that are flat-
tering but uncomfortable because we want our
partner to think we're still attractive. We swal-
low our irritation when he forgets to put the
milk back in the fridge *again*, even though we've
reminded him fifteen times – after all *we're not*

*their mothers** – because it's exhausting to be constantly complaining about trivial things. We bite our tongues in conversation so as not to contradict him and make him feel uncomfortable, or because we lack confidence in our own opinions. We grudgingly agree to sexual practices that make us feel uncomfortable, because we know we're supposed to spice up the relationship; or alternatively we keep quiet about our own desires, bury our fantasies, so as not to shatter the respectable image that women are supposed to project.

---

* It's odd how this expression comes up so often in narratives of heterosexual relationships. It's the *cri du cœur* of women who have to deal with man-children incapable of taking responsibility, their rejection of this maternal role that has no place in a relationship between adults and yet which so many men seem to seek. But at the same time it's also a way of blaming his mother for not having done a better job in bringing up her son. But what about his father? And indeed what about the adult man, who's perfectly capable of assuming his responsibilities?

We cannot truly be ourselves when our internal cursor is governed not by what our heads and our hearts tell us, but by the arbitrary opinion not of one man but of a whole crowd of men who come and go throughout our lives.

For a while now my guiding wisdom in life has been Canadian writer Sarah Hagi's *Daily Prayer to Combat Impostor Syndrome*: 'God give me the confidence of a mediocre white dude'. Whenever I'm beset by doubt, I think about all the mediocre men* who've managed to make their mediocrity pass for competence, by that magical sleight of hand called arrogance. The audacity of this ploy – the antithesis of imposter syndrome – is entirely the preserve of men. It's enraging how we're constantly terrorised at the thought of putting forward arguments in case we get the statistics wrong, or haven't read enough around a subject to have the authority

---

* You know exactly who I'm talking about.

to talk about it, or don't think we have the right level of education or experience to apply for a job. It's beyond infuriating when mediocre men, with their bullshit and inflated egos, take the place of people who are far more talented. Women have been brought up to doubt themselves constantly, while men grow up full of confidence, however way off base that may be in reality – or at the very least they're extremely good at concealing their shortcomings. There was an exasperating piece of research done by LinkedIn that showed that when a man sees a job advertised he's likely to 'give it a go' and 'see how it turns out', while women 'tend not to apply unless they're sure they're really cut out for the post'.[8]

There's a moral to this story, and an ideal we should all be working towards: we have to stop putting ourselves down, be bolder, and always, *always* ask ourselves, whenever we're overcome by doubt: *What would the mediocre white dude do?*

Having the same level of confidence in ourselves as a mediocre man has in himself would also mean being kinder to ourselves. Given the way so many men manage to bulldoze their way through the world without remotely approaching perfection in any domain, perhaps it's time to give ourselves a break as well. Where are the men so riddled with guilt they can't sleep because they left their child with their partner to go on a business trip? Where are the men who spend two weeks dwelling on a disagreement with a work colleague because they're worried they were too forthright? I'm not saying we should stoop to the lousy level of interpersonal relationships typical of most men. Just that it's time to stop guilt-tripping ourselves for failing to be a cross between Wonder Woman and a saint: time we allowed ourselves to be flawed human beings. Standards are very low for men, and far too high for women. Let's reserve ourselves the right to be ugly, badly dressed, vulgar, mean, bad-tempered, untidy, exhausted, selfish, incompetent . . .

Once we stop automatically according men importance, we'll at last behold their profound incompetence and dare to push past them. Unmoved by their ploys, we'll finally be able to take the place we deserve, which ought to be ours as a matter of right.

The heterosexuality trap

The diktat of heterosexuality is so pernicious that, not content with pushing us exclusively into relationships with men, it enjoins us to engage in such relationships for no good reason. Yes, of course, there's love – I'm hardly in a position to deny its existence. But love is not, and never has been, the only factor in the process that pushes people into becoming a couple.

Girls and boys are conditioned from an early age: even little children are expected to have a sweetheart. At an age when the expression makes no sense, the question rings out: 'Have you got a boyfriend?' At the age of four, 'having a boyfriend' (or a girlfriend) means nothing other than that: 'possessing' someone you give that title to, whom you can have for yourself in a way that's completely irrational rather than anchored in anything concrete. We teach children from a very young age that not having a girlfriend or boyfriend is almost a problem – but happily, we also let them understand that there's 'still time'. But we never give them the option of *not wanting* one. With girls, it's reinforced by an armada of clichés and conventions conveyed through the fairy stories they absorb, from the sleeping beauty waiting for a kiss from a prince to be brought back to life, to the lonesome wicked witch who devours other people's children. Boys, meanwhile, grow up with a more nuanced vision, thanks to a fantasy world peopled by solitary heroes who achieve extraordinary things because of their superpowers. The message is fundamentally the same, but boys have more opportunities to develop different perspectives. They're not so bound to this image of themselves trapped in a depressing and inert solitude. Their sense of self-worth is not conditioned by the fact of having a girlfriend or a wife. They're encouraged to be actors in a turbulent life, to reach for their dreams, to give their all to reach the top of the mountain. Little girls, meanwhile, must wait for their Prince Charming to turn up. Later, when they get older, they'll discover that it's considered strange for a woman to make the first move in a romantic relationship. (Not to mention that it's considered scandalous for a woman to recognise and be able to express her desires.)

Women *need* to be in a couple, for a single woman doesn't have as much value in the eyes of the world as a woman who belongs to a man. We imagine single women who don't have children to be selfish and bitter, while their sisters who are married and mothers have the freedom to bestow their generosity and natural kindness. A great deal of energy is deployed in persuading a woman that being in a relationship with a man is the most advantageous thing available to her – and much of the time she allows herself to be convinced, for the spectre of the crazy cat lady looms ominously over the life a single woman.

It turns out, in fact, that single women who don't have children are the happiest demographic of all. It's not altogether surprising, if you picture a life where the only mental burden that weighs on you relates to your own self, where you don't have to deal with disappointment in a mate who fails to live up to his role as a partner. Paul Dolan, professor of behavioural science at the London School of Economics speaking about his book, *Happy Ever After*, at the 2019 Hay Festival, said:

> You see a single woman of 40, who has
> never had children – 'Bless, that's a shame,
> isn't it? Maybe one day you'll meet the
> right guy and that'll change.' No, maybe
> she'll meet the wrong guy and that'll
> change. Maybe she'll meet a guy who

makes her less happy and healthy, and die sooner.*

The fact that so many women are encouraged to throw themselves into the arms of a man is more about securing the happiness, or at any rate the peace of mind, of men. Convincing a woman that she can only be fulfilled in a straight relationship is a way of pushing her into a corner. She no longer believes in herself.

When women give themselves permission to live alone, to experience single life as a life like any other, with its shortcomings as well as its rewards, rather than as a punishment, they (re)discover that they don't actually need a man, or at least not just any man, in their lives. They relish their autonomy

---

* Sian Cain, 'Women are happier without children or a spouse, says happiness expert', *The Guardian*, 25 May 2019: https://www. theguardian.com/lifeandstyle/2019/may/25/women-happier-without-children-or-a-spouse-happiness-expert

and freedom. And when they do find a partner, it isn't because they *need* one, it's because they've met a person they genuinely want to commit to, with the intention of creating a relationship based on mutual fulfilment. Not because being single is a terrifying idea and Monsieur needs someone to wash his socks and organise his diary.

Heterosexuality is a trap – that of believing in the personal relationship as the default option, inherently normal, without questioning what it is that gives meaning to a relationship for both parties. Entering a monogamous heterosexual relationship is no more natural than wearing clothes or cycling to work in the morning. For far too long women have been duped into believing that their fulfilment is only possible with the involvement of a man, however unremarkable, lazy or dull he may be: anything rather than being alone.

No. Let's discover *joie de vivre* through and for ourselves. Let's look for good reasons to commit to a relationship, avoiding the automatic mechanism that makes us afraid of being alone. Let's build a network of solid, meaningful and sincere non-romantic relationships, so we can be loved and appreciated even if we don't have a partner. Let's learn what our limits are, what we think is acceptable and what we don't, and try to expand these limits. And because this is not about claiming that every heterosexual relationship is bound to be destructive (I'm an optimistic person), let's hope that if we're in tune with our expectations we'll have a better chance of meeting people who deserve us, for whom a romantic relationship is based – as every personal relationship should be – not on possessing and exploiting the other person, but on respect, listening and mutual support. Most of all, our partners must understand the importance of our network of female friends.

Sisters

When I was younger, I prided myself on not being like other girls. I wasn't interested in the kinds of things that are commonly considered to be 'girly', and because I wasn't comfortable in groups of girls, I tried to act cool with the boys. What better way to come across as cool than to openly despise 'those girls'? There was a particular aura around these groups of guys, and it seemed so much more exciting to be their friend. True, it didn't take me long to realise that I wasn't any more comfortable in environments that were exclusively male – the fault, perhaps, of a few men who cynically took advantage of my desire to please. All the same, the fact of dissociating myself from 'those girls' by seeking the approval of men made me a really lousy friend.

How to reconcile that deeply ingrained habit we have, of trusting men and wanting to please them, with reality? We all know at least one woman who has been the victim of some kind of sexual assault. We can't be good friends to the women in our circle if we allow the men to remain on their quite undeserved pedestals. If we persist in idealising men, then however hard we try, and with all the goodwill in the world, there will always be a discrepancy between what our female friends should be able to expect from us and what we can actually offer them.

From now on I've decided that my priority is to commit to being a genuine ally to the women I know. I want them to feel safe in my company, to know that if they are ever the victim of any kind of sexual harassment or assault, I'll always be there for them. I'll always believe them, I'll never for a moment doubt the truth of anything they tell me in confidence. I'll never try to minimise what they've gone through, or impute any responsibility to them, even if – especially if – I know the attacker. I want to tell them they'll never have reason to fear that I'll find an excuse for him, or that I've set my heart on staying in touch with him. I refuse to be one of those people who thinks that domestic assault, for example, is a question of 'perspective', or a private matter between the two parties.

This priority, to be a trusted friend for women, has become a matter of urgency, and not only in cases of trauma, not only in the darkest of situations. I have made sisterhood my compass. I have a circle of radiant, talented, passionate, extraordinarily spirited female friends, who deserve all my support and all my love. I've chosen to devote to them – to all women – all my relational energy. Men don't need me in order to feel validated, convinced of their life choices, or confident of their merits. And there's a reciprocity in female relationships that goes without saying. I know I can count on every one of my female friends who's ever asked me to give up my time to help them. I know that if ever I'm demoralised or filled with self-doubt, or if something serious were to happen to me that I couldn't deal with on my own, I just need to pick up the phone and I'll have all the support I need from this group of women.

I can't say the same for the men I know, even though some of the men I know are perfectly nice. Their sympathy has limits, and so does their capacity for listening and caring. Men always want to find a solution, sort out my problems, rationalise my pain, when very often all I need is a kindly ear and a shoulder to cry on. I sometimes wonder if this male tendency to position oneself as a purveyor of solutions – as a saviour – isn't in fact an attempt, however unconscious, to get me to shut up.

For so long I allowed men to take precedence. They'd take up so much of my time without giving me much in return; expect me to be constantly bettering myself in their eyes, without making any effort to better themselves in mine. I came to the realisation that however much space I afforded them in my life, I'd never be a priority for them. Other men were held in far greater esteem than I would ever be. So now I've decided to privilege women, in the books I read, the films I watch, the culture I imbibe, and in my close friendships, so that men just aren't that important any more. Instead I privilege this sisterhood, which is so supportive, which nourishes me – in my creativity, my radicalism, my thinking both about myself and about society – in so many areas of my life, where, I've finally realised, I have no need of men to shape the person I am.

In praise of book clubs, pyjama parties and girls' nights out

Gatherings of women are like a witches' Sabbath.

When they're apolitical, men think they're frivolous and absurd. When they become sites for struggle they are exclusionary and threatening. Either way, men go to great lengths to stop them taking place. Meanwhile, though they're scandalised by accounts of what takes place in women-only spaces, men (particularly the most privileged) have never, for as long as they've had power, relinquished their right to organise gatherings from which women, and anyone else who doesn't fit in, are excluded. These are the men who want to be invited to every event, freeloaders who gatecrash parties without considering whether it's polite, whether it's the done thing to turn up without having been invited. These are the men who can't bear to be excluded from our spaces, even when they have no business being there.

The toxic masculinity that oppresses us is forged in closed male circles. From football clubs to fraternities in American universities, to elite dining societies like Oxford University's Bullingdon Club (and their notorious French equivalents, medical school societies), and then of course most of the major governing institutions all over the world, it's when men are allowed to get together among themselves that they develop their worst characteristics. To listen to them, you'd think they just partied, had a good time together, offered each other mutual support. But the truth is, they're honing their virility as a way to extend their power and consolidate their networks, in a great big cockfight. Or rather a gigantic corrida, because of course they're never the ones who are injured in the process. The scorn of women and minorities is a small price to pay for membership of this boys' club. Nothing can happen to them, or almost nothing.

Even as they cultivate their toxic and circumscribed men-only exclusivity, they want to deprive us of ourselves and our kindred spirits. When they express outrage at our feminist meetings in single-sex spaces, what they're really complaining about is the idea of us coming together as a political body, and that they have no say in the matter. It's not so much the fact of us getting together that horrifies them: knitting clubs, dinners with mums from school, book clubs, nothing could interest them less. What they can't bear, what terrifies them in fact, is the idea of us organising, coming together, forming a political entity from which ideas and plans of action will emerge. And that we attach no importance to them.

Men ridicule and scorn our 'girls' nights out', as if they're merely an expression of the essence of feminine frivolity – as if drinking whisky and playing poker were intellectually more impressive. But actually these get-togethers are far from trivial. Our knitting clubs and pyjama parties are fun, but they're also important.

Because female solidarity is never frivolous, it's always political. Nowadays we proclaim it loud and clear, and write it on our placards, not because it's new, but to bring it out of the shadows, to reclaim what's been happening for as long as men have excluded us. They want to keep us apart from each other, and in doing so to keep us out of the public arena and the political sphere. In the past they did it openly; now they do it surreptitiously, belittling our get-togethers with our women friends, poking fun at our meetings, trying to make us believe that their company ought to suffice and satisfy us.

It's in our women-only spaces that we cultivate our sisterhood. Maybe we're superficial and light-weight, perhaps we chat about clothes, cooking, makeup. It's not because such things are considered female pursuits that they're bad and we should have to give them up. It's not because men think baking is inconsequential that we should have to stop doing the things we enjoy, in the name of our liberation. Behind this apparent superficiality, brave undertakings are being put into action.

We have the power to create spaces and times in our lives where we do not serve the interests of men. Where they merely float in the air, just beyond our field of vision, and only if we summon them. Where we're free to say whatever we like about them, and also the opposite: not to talk about them at all, to make space for every other subject in the world and in our lives. Where we know we'll find the metaphysical nourishment we so desperately need, because these 'no man's lands' are zones where our fears, our joys and our anger have the right to exist. And most importantly of all, where we refuse to be divided, in a world that wants women to exist purely in opposition to each other.

Women, let's join forces! Our combined strength is formidable and fearsome.

I believe we mustn't be afraid to rouse and express our misandry. Hating men and all they represent is absolutely our right. It's also a celebration. Who would have thought there was so much joy in misandry? It's a state of mind that doesn't make us bitter or lonely, contrary to what the patriarchy would have us believe. I believe that hating men opens the door to love of women (and of ourselves) in all the forms it might take. And that we need that love – that sisterhood – in order to be truly free.

References

1 Haut Conseil à l'Égalité entre les Femmes et les
   Hommes, *Repères statistiques* (nd), see https://
   haut-conseil-egalite.gouv.fr/violences-de-genre/
   reperes-statistiques/
2 Stop Violences Femmes, *Chiffres de référence sur les
   violences faites aux femmes* (nd): https://stop-violences-
   femmes.gouv.fr/leschiffres-de-reference-sur-les.html
3 Stop Violences Femmes, *La lettre de l'Observatoire
   des violences faites aux femmes n° 13 – Novembre 2018.
   Les violences au sein du couple et les violences sexuelles en
   France en 2017* (November 2018): https://arretonsles
   violences.gouv.fr/sites/default/files/2020-07/ONVF%
   20n%C2%B013%20violences_au_sein_du_couple_
   et_violences_sexuelles_novembre_2018.pdf
4 Stop Violences Femmes, *Violences au sein du couple et
   violences sexuelles. Indicateurs annuels 2018* (November
   2019): https://arretonslesviolences.gouv.fr/sites/
   default/files/2020-04/Synthe%CC%80se_Violences
   %20au%20sein%20du%20couple%20et%20
   violences%20sexuelles_novembre%202019.pdf

5 Encyclopédie Universalis, *Pédophilie. Données statistiques du phénomène en France* (nd): https://www.universalis.fr/encyclopedie/pedophilie/5-donnees-statistiques-du-phenomene-enfrance/

6 N. Renard, 'Les attributs du pouvoir et leur confiscation aux femmes. Le genre et l'espace' (9 April 2012): https://antisexisme.net/2012/04/09/le-genre-et-lespace/

7 D. Leportois, 'Le couple ou les convictions, une féministe hétéro aura difficilement les deux' (7 October 2019): http://www.slate.fr/egalites/le-feminisme-lepreuve-du-couple-hetero/episode-1-repartition-inequitable-taches-genre

8 P. Duport, 'Offres d'emploi: les femmes postulent moins souvent que les hommes' (15 May 2019): https://www.francetvinfo.fr/replay-radio/c-est-mon-boulot/offres-d-emploi-lesfemmes-postulent-moins-souvent-que-leshommes_3425639.html

Acknowledgements

When Coline and Martin suggested I write this book they gave me the opportunity to fulfil my childhood dream. I am profoundly grateful to them for their advice and observations, for our rich conversations, and for their confidence in me. I'd like to pay tribute to Anaïs: without her, I'd probably never have started writing seriously, and it's been valuable beyond compare to have her as both friend and writing partner. I send love to Lucie, who read the beginning of this book and brought her generous but eagle eye to bear on it – and who is also, of course, a wonderful friend. Many thanks to my sister Mariane, always there to save me from my existential panic (of which I had plenty while writing this book), and of whom I'm so very proud.

I'd also like to thank from the bottom of my heart my friends Laetitia, Nepsie, Béné and Sarah, whose enthusiasm and support helped me, on a regular basis, find faith in my own words. Big love to the brilliant group of women who helped keep me sane during lockdown: our digital girls' club was a blessing. To the women of L'Échappée, a collective tackling sexual harassment and violence, I send my admiration: your commitment, courage and radicalism, as well as your kindness and generosity, both as individuals and as a group, are a permanent source of inspiration.

My gratitude and love to Mathieu, for having been the first of the two of us to believe in me.

And, of course, thanks to Eleven for being the most adorable cat on earth, my lighthouse in the night.

Interested in finding out more?

If you're wondering how to envisage a life that's a little less shaped by men, I've put together a short list of works in different media that challenge male hegemony with varying degrees of subtlety. Many of these books, TV series and films also focus on strong and unique female friendships. Coincidence? I suspect not.

BOOKS

The Nowhere Girls by Amy Reed

A young adult novel that highlights the passion of young women today fighting what seems to be societal inertia. This striking book deals with rape culture and issues linked to sexuality in general.

Witches by Mona Chollet (in French)

A paean to solitude and sisterhood, to being one's own woman, to growing older serenely, rejecting motherhood, and drawing on ancestral knowledge. Let's all be witches together!

Into the Forest by Jean Hegland

This post-apocalyptic novel, published in 1996, offers a glimpse into a world without men or capitalism, close to nature and to sisterhood. It's not all perfect, but it does perhaps portray a world in which there's a touch more kindness.

My Life on the Road by Gloria Steinem

The autobiography of one of the great figures of American feminism, who not only cultivated her independence from men but also her relationships with other women. An excellent opportunity to retrace the history of feminism.

TV SERIES

Sex Education

A bunch of young women, all with strong characters, burst onto the screen. They blossom thanks
to their beautiful, meaningful friendships. The boys,
meanwhile, learn to communicate and to be genuine, both with themselves and with other people.

Jane the Virgin

In the course of its five seasons, *Jane the Virgin* portrays several wonderful female relationships. The
series also portrays an unusual ecosystem where
men are allowed to feel and express their emotions.

GLOW

Based on the true story of *Gorgeous Ladies of
Wrestling*, this series and its incredible cast of
women challenges ideas about motherhood, marriage, ambition, independence, dreams – questions
at the heart of what it is to be a woman.

FILMS

Portrait of a Lady on Fire

Céline Sciamma creates a world in which men are seen only from afar, a lesbian love story that is also a story about sisterhood. A trio of women support each other on an island cut off from the rest of a world in turmoil.

Fried Green Tomatoes

The film adaption of the novel by Fannie Flagg tells the story of a friendship between women in 1920s Alabama, and the quest for meaning of a housewife trapped in a loveless marriage.

L'une chante, l'autre pas

Like all Agnès Varda's films, *L'une chante, l'autre pas* (*One Sings, the Other Doesn't*) is a miniature masterpiece. During the 1970s, the fight to decriminalise abortion is embodied by a group of women whose fight for women's rights leads them

into profound challenges and enduring friend
ships.

Mad Max: Fury Road

In a different register, this episode of the post-
apocalyptic saga, best known for its cast of virile
male characters, focuses on Furiosa, a woman
with a suggestive name who's fighting to save her
people. Max, meanwhile, must have about eight
lines of dialogue: what could be more perfect.